MW00801050

Conversations

Developing An Intimate Dialogue With God

ROBERT L. WAGNER

WESTBOW°
PRESS
A DIVISION OF THOMAS NELSON
& ZONDERVAN

All Scripture quotations in this book, except those noted otherwise,
are from The Holy Bible, English Standard Version®, copyright
© 2001 by Crossway Bibles, a publishing ministry of Good
News Publishers. Used by permission. All rights reserved.

Cover Designed: Marcus Raven (alefthree.com)

WestBow Press books may be ordered through booksellers or by contacting:

WestBow Press
A Division of Thomas Nelson & Zondervan
1663 Liberty Drive
Bloomington, IN 47403
www.westbowpress.com
1 (866) 928-1240

ISBN: 978-1-4908-4621-7 (sc)
ISBN: 978-1-4908-4623-1 (hc)
ISBN: 978-1-4908-4622-4 (e)

Library of Congress Control Number: 2014913406

Printed in the United States of America.

WestBow Press rev. date: 08/13/2014

To Mom and Dad for teaching me both doctrine and application of prayer. Your modeling throughout my life has resonated loud and clear.

To "Wifey," I love you for your belief and support in me. You are my inspiration. Let's build something great for the kingdom together!

CONTENTS

INTRODUCTION

Much can be said about the topic of prayer; however, this book is designed to give a brief survey concerning prayer, biblical examples of that survey, prayer starters to assist in your daily conversation time, and devotionals. It is my prayer that the contents of this book spark the desire for you to explore further.

Father, "Let the words of my mouth and the meditation of my heart be acceptable in your sight, O LORD, my rock and my redeemer!" (Psalm 19:14 English Standard Version)

Some people think that a prayer is about making a wish. They think it's about getting exactly what they want from God. However, as with everything in this life, prayer is designed to bring God glory. Prayer is about God being made known in the life of the one communicating with Him.

The bible doesn't seem to give a direct definition to prayer, but it is full of references to it. Prayer as defined by Easton's Bible Dictionary is conversing with God. The intercourse of the soul with God; not in contemplation or meditation, but in direct address to Him.

Because it shows His desired involvement in the affairs of His children; the biblical teaching of prayer emphasizes the character of God. Prayer also presupposes a belief in the personality of God, His ability and willingness to hold conversation with us, His sovereignty over everything and concern with the affairs of His creation.

Quotes about Prayer

Prayer is simply a two-way conversation between you and God. - Billy Graham

Prayer covers the whole of man's life. There is no thought, feeling, yearning, or desire, however low, trifling, or vulgar we may deem it, which if it affects our real interest or happiness, we may not lie before God and be sure of sympathy. - Henry Ward Beecher

The purpose of prayer is to get God's will done. - Samuel Gordon

Daily prayer for daily needs- E.M. Bounds

All true prayer must be offered in full submission to God - D.L. Moody

Make no decision without prayer - Elizabeth George

The essence of prayer is simply talking to God as you would to a beloved friend - without pretense or flippancy. - John Macarthur

SECTION 1

CONVERSATION IGNITED

CHAPTER 1

CONVERSATION

Prayer is simply the vehicle by which we communicate with God, a silent or spoken conversation we have with the Father. When communication takes place, it's about giving and receiving information, so prayer is all about conversation

Whether offered silently or spoken, whether constant or coincidental, whether formal or informal, prayer should be offered sincerely to God through faith. Prayer is the believer's ACTS (adoration, confession, thanksgiving, supplication) directed to the Father and, in return, listening to His response.

One may ask, "How does God speak to us?" God speaks to us through impressions of the heart, His audible voice (although this rarely happens), His vessels (e.g., preachers, believers), and Scriptures.

Often as we are reading the Scriptures, God initiates the conversation by speaking to us through the pages of His Word, and it's up to us to respond via prayer. It's when we respond through prayer that we complete this communication cycle.

The word *prayer* throughout Scripture seems to be exclusive to humans. The Bible speaks of other created beings being able to communicate with God (e.g., Job 1:6–7; Rev. 5:8–14) but never classifies these instances as prayer. Maybe there's an element of helplessness caused by our inferiority or being marred by sin that creates the need to communicate with God and request His help in matters. Prayer, as seen through Scriptures, can be viewed as the following:

- Communion with God (Phil. 4:4–7)
- Coming to God with praises and petitions (Eph. 1:15–23)
- Talking and listening to God (1 Sam. 3:2–14)
- Conscious dependence on God (2 Cor. 1:9–11)
- Acknowledgement of our need for God (1 Sam. 1:9–17)
- Calling on God to intervene in our lives (2 Sam. 15:31)
- One way God makes His will known (Col. 1:9)
- Claiming God's promises and relying on His mercy, grace, and provision (Dan. 9:17–19)

Biblical History of Prayer

The Bible first mentions prayer in the book of Genesis. We see in this part of Scripture the Earth being populated. Furthermore, after Abel's death, Adam and Eve bore another son, Seth, who was seen as the provision from God. Seth's son Enosh began to call on the name of the Lord or worship and communicate with God. Thereafter, worship of Yahweh advanced, and we see the first time the word *pray* is used in Scriptures (Gen. 18:3) and *prayer* (2 Sam. 7:27).

Throughout Scripture, we see various incidents that sparked men to pray. One of the melting pots of prayers offered to God is the Psalms. In Psalm 6, we see prayer in the time of distress; in Psalm 9, we see a prayer of thanksgiving to God. Psalm 13 is a prayer of one in sorrow, whereas Psalm 19 is a praise of God's glory. Psalm 54 contains a confident prayer in a time of distress, and according to Psalm 62, prayer is an affirmation of trust in God; however, Psalm 63 displays the need and longing for God.

It seems that prayer has been the tool everyone who has ever desired to make contact with God uses regardless of when or where one experiences this desire. It's through these ACTS of communication that we enter into a dialogue with God.

Types of Prayer

Throughout the years, believers have remembered the types of prayer through a mnemonic that describes each one: ACTS. As mentioned previously, this stands for adoration, confession, thanksgiving, and supplication.

Adoration

If someone always came to you with a request and never gave thanks for what you did for him or her, how would you feel? The first type of prayer, in accordance with the progression by which we enter into conversation with God, begins with giving adoration or praise to the Father.

Scripture is filled with prayers of praise and/or prayers that begin with praise before a request is made. Jesus models this

3

with a prayer known by many as the Lord's Prayer, though I call it the Disciple's Prayer since the Lord is teaching the disciples how to pray. (Note: The Lord's Prayer can be found in John 17, whereby the Lord prayed.) In this prayer, found in Matthew 6:9–13, Jesus began by giving adoration: "hallowed be thy name" or "holy is your name." Praise is verbally giving adoration to God's greatness, goodwill, and grace. In Psalm 150, the psalmist states, "Praise Him for His mighty acts and excellent greatness."

The Bible is filled with prayers of adoration, or praise to God. This is especially seen in the Psalms.

A Few Points about Adoration

1. Adoration should be offered from the soul with your entire heart (Ps. 9:1; 103:1; 111:1; 138:1).
2. Adoration should be expressed verbally. (Ps. 51:15; 63:3; 119:7; 171).
3. Adoration is given joyfully (Ps. 63:5; 98:4).
4. Adoration is offered continuously (Ps. 35:28; 71:6).
5. Adoration is fitting because God deserves our praise (Ps. 33:1; 147:1).

Biblical Examples of Adoration

1. Hannah (1 Sam. 2:1–10)
2. David (Ps. 119:164)
3. Anna (Luke 2:36–38)
4. Paul and Silas (Acts 16:25)

Confession

As we survey God's character, we see that He is a forgiving God. Although He has forgiven us of our past, present, and future sins, unconfessed sin can disrupt our sweet intimacy with the Lord. That's why we confess our sins privately and sometimes publicly when applicable (e.g., some illness that appears to be caused by unconfessed sins [James 5:16]). Because God is holy, we should approach Him boldly yet with reverence and vulnerability.

A Few Points about Confession

1. It should be done humbly (Isaiah 64:5–6).
2. The Bible encourages it (James 5:16; Josh. 7:19).
3. We should let go of the confessed sin and not cling to it (Prov. 28:13).

Biblical Examples of Confession

1. David (Psalm 51)
2. Nehemiah (Neh. 1:6–7)
3. Peter (Luke 5:8)

Thanksgiving

Along with adoration, giving thanks is imperative. Paul writes, "Give thanks in all circumstances; for this is the will of God in Christ Jesus for you" (1 Thess. 5:18). Just as our Father loves to answer our prayers (sometimes in ways we don't want), He also loves to hear the words *thank you.*

A Few Points about Thanksgiving

1. It's God's will (1 Thess. 5:18).
2. It should be offered before meals (Acts 27:35).
3. It should be included in our prayers (Phil. 4:6; Col. 4:2).
4. It should be offered to the godhead (Father, Son, and Spirit) (Ps. 50:14; 1 Tim. 1:12).

Biblical Examples of Thanksgiving

1. David (1 Chron. 29:10–13)
2. Jesus (Matthew 11:25–26)
3. Paul (Col. 1:3–11)
4. Angels and saints: Revelation 7:11–12

Supplications

Coming to God in conversation can be seen as we give adoration, confess sins, give thanks, and ask for things for ourselves or others. The prayer of supplication is asking God for something and is usually seen in Scripture as petitions or requests.

Inquiry prayers are when we ask God for information. When these types of prayers are offered to God in Scripture, it's to request an answer concerning personal distress or discomfort. In Joshua 7:6–9, an inquiry prayer was offered because Joshua was stunned by defeat, and he kept with the ancient ritual of mourning by tearing his clothes, putting dust on his head, and falling before God's presence until evening. In Isaiah 45:11, an inquiry supplication was offered to God because of problems understanding God's Word.

Prayers of inquiry were also offered by Job (7:11–21) because of his discomfort and questioning why God hadn't answered his prayers (23:3–5). Inquiry is also found throughout the Psalms (e.g., 2:1; 10:1; 13:1; 22:1).

A lesson I've learned as a result of Scripture and through personal experience is that God doesn't rebuke our sincere questions when our faith experience challenges Him, yet He isn't obligated to always give us the answer we desire when we desire it.

Petitions, which are similar to inquiries, are prayers calling on God to act on our behalf concerning something. An investigation of petitions throughout Scripture displays diverse and widespread requests by men and women. Just as we see in any prayer, God isn't obligated to grant our requests, but He doesn't rebuke us for asking them sincerely and with pure motives. One thing we can be sure of is that not asking means not receiving (James 4:2).

Lastly, we see prayers of supplications in the form of intercessions. How often has someone asked you to pray for him or her? When a believer offer petitions for God to act on behalf of someone else, this is called intercession. According to Scripture, we aren't only encouraged to offer prayers on behalf of others (1 John 5:16), we're also commanded to do this (1 Tim. 2:1).

This type of prayer is also common in the Psalms as shown in the examples given earlier. Intercessions were also seen in times of famine (2 Sam. 2:1) and discomfort (Job 7:11–21). Scripture displays countless people for which we should intercede: children (1 Sam. 1:27), friends (Job 42:7–8), the sick (James 5:14), our enemies (Matt. 5:44), those in authority (1 Tim. 2:1–2), and (by ministers) for parishioners (Phil. 1:4).

Another lesson concerning inquiries is that, as with other types of prayers, God doesn't rebuke our sincere questions when our faith experience challenges. However, it may be in these moments when Jesus' prayer echoes in the distance: "I am praying for them. I am not praying for the world but for those whom you have given me, for they are yours" (John 17:9–13).

A Few Things for Which We Can Pray

1. The Spread of the Gospel (Col. 4:3; 2 Thess 3:1)
2. Deliverance from Satan and evil men (2 Thess. 3:2)
3. Wisdom, strength, comprehension and encouragement (Eph 3:14-16, 18-19)
4. Knowledge of God's will with all spiritual understanding (Col. 1:9)
5. Physical and spiritual healing (James 5:13-16)
6. Those in authority (1 Tim. 2:1-2)
7. Pray about all things in every situation (1 Thess 5:16-18)

A Few Biblical Examples of Supplications

1. Abraham - Genesis 18:23-32 (Intercession)
2. Lot - Genesis 19:18-21 (Petitions)
3. Job - Job 7:11-21 (Inquiry)
4. Daniel 9:3-19 (Intercession)
5. Thief On Cross - Luke 23:39-43 (Supplication)
6. Jesus - Luke 22:32 (Intercession)

Strategic Prayer

When facing anything in life, having a strategy seems most effective in accomplishing things. Since being strategic proves to be valuable, here are five ways we can be strategic as it pertains to prayer.

- Be **Spontaneous**
  Spontaneity in prayer requires a willingness to abandon your own agenda and adopt God's agenda. It means being flexible and surrendering to whatever He permits no matter what comes your way.

- Be **Specific**
  We should feel confident as we approach the throne of grace boldly to obtain grace and find help in our time of need (Heb. 4:16). Because of such access we can be direct and specific with God (Matt. 6:7).

- **Summon** The Right Way
  When we approach God and ask Him for something, it implies that we have a need that we want to be met. Ask yourself:
  - Is my request fair and helpful to everyone concerned?
  - Is my request in agreement with the Word of God?
  - Will it draw myself and others closer to God?
  - What is my part in answering this prayer?

- **Supplicate** with all your heart
  - pray aloud
  - write down distractions
  - keep a prayer journal

- Never **Stop** Praying - 1 Thess 5:17
  Praying without ceasing doesn't mean never ceasing to break our communication, but rather having a persistence or regularity in our conversation to the Father.

The image below is a picture of my hand and it serves as a strategic way to pray. It is a guide for those I pray for. It is something I've seen for years and have adopted in my personal prayer times often. I am not sure the originator of this, but it is a blessing in aiding me in whom to pray for by simply using each finger as my prayer guide.

Thumb: Pray for those closest to your heart such as family and friends.

Index/Pointer Finger: Pray for those that point you to truth such as your pastor, mentors and ministers.

Middle Finger: Pray for the leaders of the church, locally and globally. Also, pray for leaders of government.

Ring Finger: Pray for those in trouble, persecuted and/or in pain.

Pinky Finger: Pray for those unnoticed, abused, orphaned and deprived.

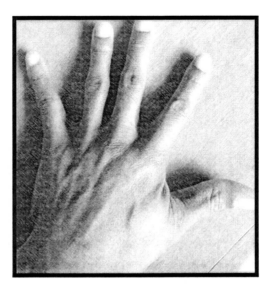

Key Benefits to Prayer

Prayer is vital to the growth of the believer. It pumps up our faith in God's faithfulness (Acts 27:21-26) and produces boldness for Christ by purifying our motives for ministry service (Acts 4:23-24, 29-31). The common thought among believers is that "prayer changes things," however prayer doesn't always change circumstances. If we surrender to God's will, prayer can change our perspective to trust God's providence. When believers fail to pray it results in that believer's loss, because nothing can replace the joy of communing with the Father. It should be our first response instead of our last resort (Acts 12:1-5).

Therefore a believer should devote himself to prayer (Col. 4:2), by humbly seeking the face of God with all his heart (2 Chron. 7:14-15) and asking according to His will (1 John 5:14-15) with fervor both regularly and persistently (1 Thess 5:17; Acts 2:42; James 5:16).

Praying In the Spirit

"praying always with all prayer and supplication in the Spirit, being watchful to this end with all perseverance and supplication for all the saints -" (Eph. 6:18)

This verse has been used to support speaking in tongues while praying, namely "praying in the spirit." Often people use the statement, "speak in tongues so that Satan can't hear you pray to God." My question is, "are you saying Satan is so powerful that he can hear what you say to God and stop whatever God wants to do on your behalf?" There is much to say about the topic of tongues, but that is for another book or teachable moment. However, this Scripture doesn't imply that we are to speak in tongues when we are praying, but rather our reliance upon God when we do pray. This verse highlights the general prayer life of the believer, by focusing on the variety of prayers (i.e. "prayer and supplication"), the frequency by which we pray (i.e. "always"), in whom we should have faith in as we pray (i.e. "in the Spirit"), the fashion by which we pray (i.e. "being watchful"), the fullness of time we should endeavor in praying (i.e. "all perseverance") and for whom (i.e. "all the saints"). It has been said, "we pray to the Father, in the name of Jesus and by means, or in the power of the Holy Spirit."

Prayer and Fasting

"Fasting helps express, deepen, confirm the resolution that we are ready to sacrifice anything, even ourselves to attain what we seek for the kingdom of God. - Andrew Murray

"So He said to them, 'This kind can come out by nothing but prayer and fasting'." (Mark 9:29 - New King James Version)

Many people believe that fasting is good for the purpose of purifying the body, while see it beneficial for physical and/or cosmetic reasons. However, Scripture teaches a great deal about fasting, and yet none is for these practical reasons. Also the scriptures seems to only command fasting as it pertained to the children of Israel observing the Day of Atonement (Lev. 16:29; 23:27), which was a national fast that included adults to children.

What is fasting?

The Greek word for fasting means to not eat, or abstain from food. Fasting is the voluntary withdrawal of food for a period and can include a partial fast (i.e. Daniel 1) or ultimate fasting (i.e. Jesus - 40 days).

Purpose of Fasting

We find tucked away in the book of Isaiah 58, nine key things that display the purpose for fasting.

- to loose the bonds of wickedness (v. 6a)
- to undo the heavy burdens (v. 6b)
- to let the oppressed go free (v. 6c)
- to break every yoke (v. 6d)
- meet physical needs (v. 7)
- clear insight in decisions (v. 8a)
- for health reasons and healing (v. 8b)
- righteous life and influence (v. 8c)
- for the glory of the Lord to protect us (v. 8d)

Benefits and Dangers of Fasting

Fasting as a spiritual discipline can be very beneficial to the believer. I believe that it makes our heart more attentive to God and demonstrates our seriousness. Fasting also allows more time for us to converse with the father, however if you are fasting and not entering into conversation you are merely exercising a good diet.

Along with benefits, fasting also has its potential dangers such as trying to manipulate God. We see this in Isaiah 58:1-5 whereby the people seem to show an outward eager to hear from God, but they were quarreling and having poor relationships with others. They were going through the motions thinking God would see them, not realizing God saw their motives and exploitation. Fasting can also be potentially dangerous when people attempt to impress others by doing so. I see so often people who enter into fast and post on social media, tell others what they are doing, when Jesus clearly states in Matthew 6:16-18 the proper way to fast. Lastly, a person can become legalistic in that they think this is the way to please God and be approved by God, when the way to please God is simply by faith. For without faith, it is impossible to please Him (Hebrew 11:6).

Application

Remember that prayer is not some mystical thing that only the elite engage in, but rather it is simply a conversation that we have with the Father. As with all dialogue, it is about giving and receiving information. So as you enter into a regular conversation with the Lord, remember also that fasting can be a vital part of that relationship, because it allows more time for us to enter into conversation, clears our hearts to be more attentive and confirms our seriousness to hear from the Lord. It is my prayer that this brief surveys of prayer jumpstarts your lifelong communication with the Father, thus, experiencing the joy that comes with communing with Him.

CHAPTER 2

BIBLICAL CONVERSATION EXAMPLES

It is always great to see biblical truth modeled, and scripture is full of application. This section is a brief collection of biblical prayers, promises, and postures. This is not meant to be an exhaustive look, but simply some examples to aid in your conversation time.

Public Prayers

1) Joshua (Josh. 7:6-9)
2) David (1 Chron. 29:10-19)
3) Solomon (2 Chron. 6)
4) Jehoshaphat (2 Chron. 20:5-13)
5) The Levites (Neh. 9)
6) Multitude of People (Luke 1:10)
7) First Century Believers (Acts 2:46; 4:24)
8) Peter and John (Acts 3:1)
9) Antioch Teachers and Prophets (Acts 13:1-3)
10) Paul (Acts 16:16)

Private Prayers

1) Lot (Gen. 19:20)
2) Abraham's servant (Gen. 24:9-12)
3) Jacob (Gen. 32:9-12)
4) Gideon (Judges 6:22, 36, 39)
5) Hannah (1 Samuel 1:9-10)
6) David (2 Sam. 7:18-29)
7) Hezekiah (2 Kings 20:1-3)
8) Isaiah (2 Kings 20:11)
9) Manasseh (2 Chron. 33:18-19)
10) Ezra (Ezra 9:5-6)
11) Nehemiah (Nehemiah 2:4)
12) Jeremiah (Jeremiah 32:16-25)
13) Daniel (Daniel 9:3, 7)
14) Jonah (Jonah 2:1)
15) Habakkuk (Habakkuk 1:2)
16) Jesus (Matthew 14:23; 26:36, 39)
17) Anna (Luke 2:36-37)
18) Saul (Acts 9:11)
19) Peter (Acts 9:40; 10:9)
20) Cornelius (Acts 10:30)

Physical Postures of Prayer

1) Kneeling -1 Kings 8:54
2) Standing - 1 Kings 8:22
3) Bowing Heads - Exodus 4:31
4) Face To The Ground - 2 Chronicles 20:18
5) Weeping - Jeremiah 31:9

Non-Physical Postures Of Prayer

1) Confession - Nehemiah 1:7
2) Repentance - 1 Kings 8:33
3) Humility - Genesis 18:27
4) Soberness - 1 Peter 4:7
5) Thanksgiving - Philippians 4:6
6) Persistence - Luke 11:8

Persistent Prayers

1) Jacob, wrestling with God - Genesis 32:24-30
2) Moses, for his people - Exodus 33:12-16
3) Elijah, for God to confirm His calling - 1 Kings 18:22-44
4) Roman Centurion, who implored Jesus for servant's healing - Matthew 8:5
5) Bartimaeus - Mark 10:48

Prominent Prayers in the Bible

1) Abraham's Prayer for Sodom - Genesis 18:23-25
2) Elijah's Prayer at Mount Carmel - I Kings 18:36-39
3) Solomon's Prayer of Dedication - 1 Kings 8:22-30
4) Solomon's Request For Wisdom - 1 Kings 3:4-14
5) David's Confession of Sin - Psalm 51
6) King Hezekiah's Prayer - 2 Kings 19:15-19
7) David's Prayer of Thanks - 2 Samuel 7:18-29
8) The Prayer of Jabez - 1 Chronicles 4:10
9) The Prayer of Ezra - Ezra 9:5-15
10) Hezekiah's Prayer when Sick - Isaiah 38:2-8
11) Daniel's Prayer for the Captive Jews - Daniel 9:4-19
12) Habakkuk's Prayer - Habakkuk 3:2-19

13) The Disciple's Prayer - Matthew 6:9-15
14) The Tax Collector's Prayer - Luke 18:13
15) Christ's Intercessory Prayer - John 17
16) Stephen's Prayer at His Stoning - Acts 7:59-60
17) Paul's Prayer for Spiritual Wisdom - Ephesians 1:15-23
18) Paul's Prayer for Spiritual Growth - Ephesians 3:14-21
19) Paul's Prayer for Partners in Ministry - Philippians 1:3-11
20) Paul's Prayer for Knowing God's Will - Colossians 1:9-12
21) A Prayer of Praise - Jude 1:24-25

A Few Prayer Parallels (Synonyms)

1) Looking Up - Psalm 5:3
2) Lifting Up the soul - Psalm 25:1
3) Lifting Up The Heart - Lamentations 3:41
4) Bowing The Knees - Ephesians 3:14
5) Seeking The Face Of God - Psalm 27:8
6) Crying Unto God - Psalm 34:6
7) Calling On The Name Of God - Genesis 12:8
8) Crying To Heaven - 2 Chronicles 32:20
9) Wrestle With God - Genesis 32:24
10) Pouring Out The Soul - 1 Samuel 1:15

Parables on Prayer

1) Friend At Night - Luke 11:5-8
2) Persistent Widow - Luke 18:1-8
3) Pharisee and the tax collector - Luke 18:9-14

Places to Pray

1) Mountain - Matthew 14:23
2) Solitary Place - Mark 1:35
3) In a Garden - Matthew 26:36
4) Wilderness - Luke 5:16
5) Prayer Closet - Matthew 6:6
6) In Church - 1 Corinthians 11:4

Promises Concerning Prayer

Write a one sentence statement of the promise taught in each scripture

1) 2 Chronicles 7:14
_____

2) Psalm 145:18-19
_____

3) Proverbs 15:8
_____

4) Isaiah 65:24
_____

5) Jeremiah 33:3
_____

6) Matthew 18:19
_____

7) Matthew 21:22
_____

8) John 14:13
_____

9) John 15:7
_____

10) John 16:23-24

---

11) Romans 8:26

---

12) 1 John 5:14-15

---

13) 1 Peter 3:12

CHAPTER 3

CONVERSATION STARTERS

Contained in this chapter of the book are over 200 conversation starters. The idea of writing this book developed out of the daily prayers I posted online for about 6 months. As a jumpstart to a low battery can ignite a car, I pray these conversation starters can assist in your prayer life. Each day meditate on 1 or more of these short prayers, write them down, post online, or send yourself alerts, which can serve as a great reminder to pray. Prayerfully by the end of the conversation starters your need for a boost would be no more, and you can begin your conversations without assistance.

Lord, teach us to not let our strong desire for a thing weaken our rationale in acquiring that thing.

Adonai (Lord), we ask you to attend to our appeals and astonish us with your amazing answers.

Lord, teach us how to look beyond our circumstances and look to you.

Father, help us become more rooted and grounded in your love and word, so that we may continually grow higher in our praise and adoration to you

Lord, grant us favor to meet the right people with the right resources at the right time.

Lord, help us to distinguish between present trials and future glory, for they are incomparable (Rom. 8:18)

Lord, help us to identify the drips from the faucets in our lives that become deluges, or a superabundant stream!

Father, may our faith be effective in deepening our knowledge of every good thing we share for the sake of Christ.

Lord God, may we long to become hearers and doers of your Word.

Father, may our love for the brethren and our faith in the Lord Jesus become evident to all.

Lord, help us to have a steady view of the Gospel of Christ.

Father, give strength to your people and open our eyes to the peace you have already given. (Ps 29; Gal. 5)

Father, may we not just settle for average but strive for excellence.

Father, sometimes I have a hard time making time to speak to you. Help me by strengthening my resolve to spend time with you in daily conversation.

Father, I am grateful that you know what is best for me. Help me align my thinking to your plans.

Father, teach me to pray for those I care about.

Father, thank you for hearing my prayers; I lay my desires before you.

Father, give me a renewed burden to share your words of hope to the hopeless.

Father, you are the master of my fate and the captain of my soul; therefore, I submit to whatever your will is.

Father, as long as we have breath we will praise you for your mighty acts and excellent greatness. (Ps. 150)

Father you took a man with no woman and created the first woman, and then took a woman with no man and brought forth Jesus. Therefore, I am confident you can take my situation and work it out for your good pleasure.

Father, teach us that keeping in step with your Spirit we will not fulfill fleshly desires.

Lord, as helmets sustain soldiers, we bless you for the hope of salvation that sustains us when the battle gets tough.

Lord, may we become skilled swordsman by becoming familiar with your Word as we study, search and spread your truth.

Father, help us see the value in praying fervently (and soberly) for the entire body, that we may speak boldly your Word.

Father, we are rocked by your love and grace. Thank you for being yourself despite our mess.

Father, teach us to not ourselves to the size of our problems, but rather limit ourselves to the size of You.

Father, you are wonderful, and your goodness humbles us. May we serve others like unto you.

Father, we have limitations and flaws, but that is a perfect opportunity for you to infuse your inner strength into us and use us greatly. (Phil. 4:13)

Father, in all our ways we acknowledge You, so that you can direct our paths.

Father, I woke up this morning and was rocked by your grace. Thank you for your grace, it never gets old.

Lord, grant your servants an increasing desire to gladly do your Will.

Father, may your Spirit enable us to grasp your Word as it should be grasped.

Father, may we see your hand print on things we never before realized.

Father, may our saltiness today cause others to see their spiritual dehydration and drought and be drawn to You.

Father, help us to see our losses are oftentimes preparation for a greater gain.

Father, teach us that life is fruitful when it is sacrificial

Father, help us to be quick to discern opportunities to serve.

Father, so honored to be a part of your family and a recipient of your grace

Father, teach us how to manage our time, resources, relationships and selves better.

Father, help us to not differentiate between sacred and secular, but rather seek to honor you in all things. (Col. 3:23)

Father, we yield to the work of your Spirit at work in and through us.

Father, we can only imagine what it would be like in your presence. May we live in such a way on Earth as if we were before your throne.

Father, you don't have to remove the mountains before us, however grant us wisdom to know if we should climb or walk around them.

Father, may we see things through the lenses of your Word.

Father, may the power of your love rule over what we say and do.

Father, we remember your word that declares we have not because we ask not.

Father, help us to remember to aid our brothers in carrying their heavy burdens (Gal 6:1)

Father, make us more and more into the beauty and strength of your Son's image.

Father, we praise you for your mighty acts and excellent greatness. Show up mightily in our lives today.

Father, teach us to love like you daily.

Father, may the eyes of our understanding be enlightened so that we can know you better.

Father, may we be reminded to praise you for being so awesome. In doing so, the overcast of despair will move away.

Father, because of your love for us we are not consumed, thus we shout Great Is Thy Faithfulness.

Father, you're the strength of our hearts and our portion when our flesh fails. You're our only hope; thus, we yield to you.

Father, remind us to carry our own light loads and assist our brethren with their heavy burdens through love and prayer.

Father, thank you for your grace.

Father, may we become so self less that we think of others in our prayers more than ourselves.

Lord, as you have taken us out of the night of sin and ignorance, may we remember to not sleep in spiritual indifference.

Father, may the vision, goals, and dreams which we carry leap at the sound of your voice.

Father, set us on fire so that we will be diligent in our pursuit, of those to win for you.

Father, help us to shift away the clouds of darkness and despair with songs of hope and life.

Father, if the world rejects and despises your Son, may we not seek to be honored and loved by them.

Father, whether in dark nights or bright days we praise you for the certainty of your love. May this truth comfort and warm us when our reality brings tension and cold from others.

Father, may we not be stagnant as Dead Sea Christians, but a conduit of the resources you have placed in our care.

Father, just want to say thank you!

Father, fill us up and send us out.

Father, what an awesome God you are, and we serve you gladly.

Father, you are greater, higher, and stronger than anything else. We set our focus back to you. You are incomparable!!!!

Father, as the rain showers the Earth we ask you to shower the soil of our hearts with your grace.

Father, create in me a clean heart, and refresh my attitude. (Psalm 51:10)

Father, help us to discern opportunities that present itself and redeem the time

Father, sometimes trusting is difficult but we understand it is necessary. Help us in our moments of unbelief. (Heb. 11:6)

Father, even when I am afraid I will put my trust in you (Psalm 56:3)

Father, for the anxiety that is in the heart of my family. I pray you give me a soft and timely word.

Father, we desire to be rooted deeply in you, thus, rising up in praise to you and children bearing much fruit.

Father, continue to enlighten us to the riches and freedom that are found in knowing your truth.

Father, thank you for sending your son Jesus to redeem us from the curse of the law by becoming that curse for us.

Father, thank you for sending grace and truth through your Son. May your truth lead me to a proper response to your grace.

Father, meet those today who are "stunned" by sorrow and pain. Touch! Heal! Deliver!

Father, use us to reconcile men back to you.

Father, thank you for saving, strengthening and sustaining.

Father, we bless you for healing our hurts

Father, save us from our spiritual sloth.

Lord, open the doors and windows of our soul to the Sun of Righteousness. - Charles Spurgeon

Father, we yield to the filling of your Spirit (control) in our lives today. May our speech, swagger and smell be affected.

Father, May an increasing desire be birthed in us to learn you more.

Father, may you turn your face upon us and give us peace.

Father, may we hear the sound of your music clearly, so that we can know where you're grooving and join you there.

Father, thank you that although the things that may have happened to us may not be "good" but you will work all things out for our good.

Father, thank you for love that reaches down to the undeserving. May we reciprocate the love you have for us to someone else.

Father, may we walk as children of the light and light up our various dark roads today.

Father, burn within us a hunger and thirst for biblical truth, searching diligently daily resulting in our nobility.

Father, give us our daily provision

Father, thank you for the healing that is awaiting me in this lifetime or eternity.

Father, strengthen our commitment to excellence. It's difficult but we must suffer long in order to win the ultimate prize

Father, may your Spirit continue to enlighten us to the wonderful truths found in your Word.

Father, teach us by your spirit to hide ourselves in your bosom of love.

Father, may our hearts beat for the things your heart beats for.

Father, thank you that these light and momentary afflictions are preparing us for an eternal weight of glory.

Father, help us to know fully and skillfully apply.

Lord, extend wisdom to your people and even when we don't ask for it may you slap us in the head with it.

Father, break up the fallow ground of our hearts so the seed planted can yield forth a beautiful harvest

Father, bless us and keep us, make your face shine upon us and be gracious to us.

Father, because you are creator of and have knowledge of all things, we humbly submit to your plan. Thank you that no problem is too great or too small for your attention.

Father, may your people develop the taste buds that reciprocate yours. May we love what you love and hate what you hate.

Father, our supreme desire, is to bring you honor and glory.

Father, fashion us into the beauty of your Son's image.

Father, we commit our plans to you and submit to your rearrangements.

Father, lead us not into temptation

Father, you are the light of my salvation.

Father, help us to live purposeful today and hereafter.

Father, help us to develop a constant communication with you through regular conversations throughout our day.

Father, may there be visible signs that we have come in contact with you in our walk and talk.

Father, it is great to know that no circumstance is beyond your control; therefore we can rest knowing you got it covered.

Father, we gladly offer all that we have and all that we know you know exactly what to do with each

Father, we are unashamed of the gospel of Christ both when we think it matters and in daily living.

Father, help us discern where you are creating incredible music so we can join you there and groove

O Lord, increase our gratitude so that your love may rain upon our insensible hearts.

Father, we look way above the hills to You who created them. You are the One who supplies our help. (Ps. 121)

Father, may lives be positively impacted by the words we type, talk, and walk.

Father, may we continue to use the platform you have given us to reach more for your kingdom.

Father, because we oftentimes ask for what we already have, teach us what to pray for.

Father, we yield ourselves to work of the Spirit so that the life of Christ can be lived out in us.

Father, open our eyes to the opportunities you give us to develop fruit in our lives.

Lord, I pray for the church...may we regain our saltiness in this hour.

Lord, you are my strength and you shield me from all evil.

Father, if we will know your followers by their fruit (Matthew 7), may we stop being gift inspectors and inspect fruit.

Father, I pray we have a peaceful realization of your gracious presence in our lives today

Father, we pause to declare you alone are majestic, excellent, and awesome. We stand in awe of you

Father, we are convinced that we cannot live without you. For it's in you we live, move, and have our being.

Father we take a moment out of our schedules just to say THANK YOU!!!!

Father, direct us to the bridge you have formed over every difficult river we encounter.

Father, "may it please you to bless the house of your servant..." so that we might expand our reach and influence greatly. (2 Sam 7:29)

Father, may our goal be to love and make you famous and not acquiring riches.

Lord, thank you for the vehicle of prayer. It doesn't always change circumstances, but changes us when we yield to your plans.

Father, May we be reminded of the joy of fighting for others than being consumed with ourselves when we pray

Father, may your precious Spirit breathe life into our thoughts, words, and creations.

Father, may we not be so concerned with keeping it real that we lose sight of keeping it righteous.

Father, thank you for the confidence of knowing that whatever we ask in Jesus name and for your glory will be granted.

Father, you are AWESOME!!!

Father, As I think about your goodness and meditate on you, my has become satisfied with fullness and my mouth will praise thee with joy (Psalm 63:5-6)

Lord, help us to identify the drips from the faucets in our lives that become overwhelming floods.

Father, thank you that even though weeping last throughout the night, your joy is brand new each morning (Psalm 30:5)

Father, I am very grateful for what you have allotted me. I choose not to complain

Father, help me to hold back nothing but become a minister of compassion to those in need.

Father, may our supreme desire and that which we strive for daily be to bring you glory

Father, teach us to number our days that we may get a heart of wisdom.

May the favor of the Lord be upon us, and may He establish the work of our hands to do good. (Ps. 90:17)

Father, may we act on and believe the truth of your Word today regardless of how we feel

Help me to be compassionate to those who are dealing with different degrees of stress today.

Father, so that we can stand against the tricks of the enemy, we put on the whole armor that you have provided (Eph 6:11)

May we be reminded that although we use disciplines w/ physical elements (i.e. prayer, giving) our fight is spiritual.

Lord, as the breastplate protects the soldier in close combat, help us protect our souls from attack as we live holy daily

Lord, we take up daily the basic faith in You that covers our entire being from all sorts of temptations and attacks.

Because you have been my constant help, I will praise you in the safety of your arms (Psalm 63:7)

Father, thank you for the stability that comes from the gospel and gives us calm peace in the midst of this battle.

Father, we bow our knees to you that you may grant unto us strength by your Spirit. (Eph. 3:14, 16)

Father, I pray that we grow in love for each other so that the world may know we are your disciples. (John 13:35)

Father, may we grow in fervent charity towards each other. (1 Pet. 4:8)

Father, because you are the giver of favor, one day in your presence is worth a thousand days elsewhere.(Psalm 84:10-12)

Father, without you I am nothing and can do nothing but fail.

Father, may the fruit of your spirit be evident in our lives. (Gal. 5:22-23)

Father, we believe but help our unbelief so that you can perform mighty works amongst us. (Matthew 13:58)

Father, there is nothing too hard for you. (Gen. 18:14)

Father, our faith, is in you for only you can make wars to cease across the Earth. (Ps. 46:9)

Father, guide me in the way that is pleasing to you.

Father, teach me to be generous with my time, talent, and treasures.

Father, may we not just have a form of godliness but increase in our acceptance of the power within (2 Tim 3:5)

My soul waited upon you, O God, for its from you that my salvation come. (Ps. 62:1)

Lord, we call upon you to show us great and mighty things that we not. (Jer. 33:3)

Father, my enemies may be many, but you are my shield around me, my glory, and the One who lifts my head (Psalm 3)

Father, our hearts desire, is that our brethren be saved. Give us a heart that beats for the things your beat for (Rom. 10:1)

Father we draw nigh unto you, knowing you will draw nigh unto us (James 4:8)

Father may we give ourselves continually in prayer and to the ministry of your Word. (Acts 6:4)

Father continue to rain down your blessings upon us, so that we can continue to be a blessing for you.

Father, may we preach your gospel in not only words but with the power and much assurance in the Holy Spirit. (1 Thess. 1:5)

Father, you are magnificent, and I adore you.

Father. give me a single mind to trust you completely and obey you fully.

Lord, may my life be known to bring you constant glory

Lord, teach me to number my days.

Father, I am longing and thirsty for you; I will praise you as long as I live and be fully satisfied (Psalm 63)

Lord, thank you that the power that saved me is the same power that keeps me.

Lord, teach me how to love you more.

Lord, may your peace rule my life.

Lord, may your goodness and mercy forever follow me and I will dwell in your house forever (Psalm 23)

Father, in my seasons of darkness, may the light of your Word shine bright.

God, I am lost without you.

Father, my heart is heavy, but you have turned my mourning into dancing before, now will you do it again (Psalm 30: 11)

Father, help me remember that whatever happens today is well within your ability to handle.

Lord, your thoughts, are precious to me and they are many not few. Thank you for thinking of me and giving me a future (Psalm 139: 17; Jeremiah 29:11)

Father, your hands of comfort and strength has watched over me and held me in the night.

Father, may your irresistible grace be displayed in my life towards others.

Spirit of the Lord, help me to preach the good news to the poor.

Lord, open the doors that no man can close and close the doors that no man can open.

Father, what a wondrous love you have for me that you would give your Son to die. Thank you for loving me even though I was unlovable.

Grant me Father the ability to grasp your word.

Lord, fill your servant with your Spirit that I may proclaim your truth with boldness (Acts 4:24-31)

Father, today I am praying for those who mistreat me. Continue to give me grace to showcase your love (Matthew 5:44)

Teach me Lord and guide my way.

Father, even though at times I don't see myself as you, I praise thee for I am fearfully and wonderfully made (Psalm 139:14)

Father, you are my heart and my strength.

Lord God, hold my hand in my weakness for you are my stability.

Father, may your love rest upon me, and your joy exude from me.

Lord God, I will place my trust in you whether I am afraid or not.

Father, I hope in only you, for you never let me fall.

As I begin my day, I pray you walk with me and lead me wherever you please.

May your will be done in my life this day.

Father, may your name be glorified in my actions today.

I pray you give courage to speak your truth in the midst of troubling times.

Father, help me to see where I have failed and help me to correct whatever is on me to correct.

My lips will make you known, because of your great love for me, which is better than life. (Psalm 63:3)

Father, may my heart be pure before you and my spirit steadfast (Psalm 51:10)

SECTION 2

31 DAY DEVOTIONAL

In this section contains 31 daily devotionals to aid in personal quiet time and growth with the Father. Many of these entries are a collection of blog posts I have written (In order to read full blogs visit http://robertlwagner.com)

DAY 1

A CALL TO REMEMBER
A CALL TO OBEY

Deut 1:5

Here they stand on the east side of the Jordan River, and they were poised and ready to enter the land promised to them. However, the generation that had received the instruction had passed away in the wilderness, and a new generation needed to hear clear instructions from God. The Bible then says in "Moses undertook to expound this law."

Moses begins by giving a review of how God had been faithful to their nation in the past. He spoke of the Abrahamaic covenant, Israel's faith failure yet God's continued provision. He spoke of God producing victories and a call to remember Mt Sinai. After recounting God's faithfulness during the wilderness and Israel's sins, Moses issued a charge to the people to obey the Lord.

How often are those who knew the Lord and paved the way for us departed from us and we need to hear for ourselves? No longer are the older saints who disciple us present, and we need to hear or be reminded of God's past faithfulness, but also a call to individual obedience. Remember that God rewards obedience, and there are consequences for disobedience. Also, God wants us to share with others His word and instruct them, because it is so easy to forget God in times of prosperity, especially when our leaders and teachers are with us no more.

Application:

Will you obey God? When the leaders are no longer present, will you stand up and remind others of God's faithful and charge them to obey?

DAY 2

A DAILY MEMORIAL: ULTIMATE SACRIFICE

Each year we celebrate Memorial Day, which is a celebration of recognition to all the servicemen and servicewomen who have served our country by giving their lives for our freedom. It was formerly known as Decoration Day and was first enacted by a group of Union veterans (Grand Army of the Republic) to honor men who gave their lives fighting in the Civil War. It is said that all or majority of these men were black veterans and later this holiday became a national holiday celebrating all servicemen.

Just as we celebrate our servicemen for their sacrificial acts, we celebrate daily our Lord and Savior for his sacrificial death that spans broader and deeper than national and natural freedom. Jesus made the ultimate sacrifice.

His sacrificial death was holistically voluntary. Among many who gave their lives up in our country, most gave it voluntarily. Although many gave their lives for their comrades while in foxholes and many volunteered for military duty, there have been times in our history where people have been drafted. However, Jesus' life was not taken from him, but rather He gave it up freely. Notice these four points:

[1] No one could take His life (John 19:7-12) [2] He would lay it down Himself (Matthew 27:50) [3] He had full authority to lay it down (Matthew 26:53, 54) [4] This was all according to the plan of God

His sacrificial death was holistically vicarious. Jesus took the place for you and I; He vicarious suffered for us. Scripture says, "For He made Him who knew no sin to be sin for us, that we might become the righteousness of God in Him" (2 Cor. 5:21). My father always calls this passage the great exchange.

His sacrificial death was holistically victorious. There have been those in our history who have given their lives for the freedom of individuals in our nation, yet not always through the history of our nation have all individuals experienced those freedoms. Jesus uttered three emphatic words, "It is finished." The entire work of redemption had been brought to completion; it had been paid in full. As a result, all that would place "saving faith" in Jesus would experience the victory in Him. Because

1) Jesus paid the sin debt in full (John 19:30)
2) He rose from the dead three days later (Acts. 2:23)
3) He is coming back some day as King of Kings and Lord of Lords (Heb. 9:27-28)

Thus, we remember those who have fallen serving our country on Memorial Day, however every day we remember Jesus, who died, was buried, and rose again with all power in His hand also on Memorial Day and every other day alike.

"Father, help us to remember the sacrifice daily of our Lord, and thank you for demonstrating your love towards us. Amen"

DAY 3

ATTITUDE

One of the things we fail to work on in life isn't our skills, abilities, gifts, etc. but rather it's our Attitude. Over the years I have learned the importance of attitudes. I am not sure when or how I discovered this cool trick, but I have been using it for over a decade. If we take the word Attitude and calculate it based upon each letter's position in the alphabet, we will see an amazing discovery. A-1, T-20, T-20, I-9, T-20, U-21, D-4, E-5 and if we added each of these numbers together, we would get 100. Leading groups of people from business to ministry, I realize a person's attitude affect 100% of how we respond and interact with things we come in contact with. Did you know that your attitude can lift you up or bring you down? Or did you know it can be compounded with attitude of others? Your attitude is about your character, and it overflows into your actions. I once heard a preacher say, "your attitude is an inward feeling expressed by behavior." It will be the dominant drive that will determine your success or failure. Oftentimes we stand as equals with talent and ability, but our attitude will give us a slight edge that is needed to accomplish more. It's the attitude of "the giant is so big I can't kill him" (Psalm 3:3) that will create failure, but it's the approach of "the giant is so big, the target is impossible to miss" that will generate an opportunity for success.

Application:

Will you begin to develop a good attitude? Will you see each day as an opportunity to make God famous? What is your biggest obstacle in developing the right attitude?

DAY 4

DEAD STICKS DOING BIG THINGS

Have you ever thought to yourself, "I am insignificant" or "I am limited?" Or maybe you thought of it this way, "I love The Lord and I love the fact that He saved me, but compared to so many others I am deprived of gifts and talents and insignificant to the body of Christ." Consider that the Bible has a few different perspectives, such as one body and many members (1 Cor. 12) but I want to focus our attention on something easily overlooked.

When I consider the way, God used the "rod of Moses" I am completely rocked. In the book of Exodus, God speaks to Moses from a burning bush to go proclaim to Egypt "Let my people go." After some dialogue and questioning with God, Moses' attention is brought to the thing in his hand, approximately 6 foot dead stick. A stick that he would have probably held dear for the better part of 40 years, since He was a shepherd and shepherds clung to their rods. God commands him to toss it on the ground and as he obeyed it became a serpent. As He obeyed again, he picks up the serpent by the tail and it became a rod. Immediately God tells him to go and confront Pharaoh with the rod in his hand. We know the story from here but for outline purposes:

* Aaron cast down the rod in front of Pharaoh and it became a serpent (Ex 4:16)* rod placed into the waters and turns waters into blood (Ex 7:15-17)* Moses stretches forth the rod and plagues followed (frogs, thunder and hail, etc. - Ex 8:1-10:15)* what has became a rod of judgment to the Egyptians became the rod of supply for the children of Israel as they passed through divided waters to safety (Ex 14:16)* the rod also brought military victory as it was held up (Ex 17:9)

However, through all these incredible accomplishments brought forth by a dead stick, an interesting verse is often not remembered or over-looked. It is found in Exodus 4:20 as Moses sets out for Egypt "...And Moses took the rod of God in his hand" The rod of Moses had become the rod of God. (Inserts Shout) Consider all the ways that God used this dead stick of wood, and consider how much more are you than a dead stick of wood. Though we are limited in resources, limited in talent, weak in energy, and sometimes emotionally unbalanced we are greater than a piece of wood. This rod in the hands of Moses did incredible things, and I am sure would be a great candidate for a residence in a museum somewhere, however the key is the rod of Moses became the rod of God. Thus, as we begin this year with hopes, dreams and aspirations of doing incredible things for the kingdom of God, we must remember that we too have to transform what was entrusted to us to the voice of God (singer), fingers of God (musician), pen of God (writer/author), etc. Just as the little Hebrew boy placed his 5 biscuits and 2 sardines into the hands of Jesus and it fed 5,000 men (not including the women and children), little becomes much when we put it into the Master's hands.

Application:

What do you desire to accomplish this year? How can our community of faith pray with you this year? What do you have that you liken unto the dead stick of wood in Moses' hand?

DAY 5

AND WE KNOW THAT...

"....all things work together for good to those who love God..." - Romans 8:28 (NIV)

There are four words that are often missed in this wonderful passage.... "And we know that." It is interesting to note that all things that happen to you and I aren't good things. When we experience things such as divorce, rape, or other tragedies, God is not saying that these things are good. However, in the midst of these atrocious things that we experience, what we understand is that God works these things out (whether good or bad) out for our good. We believe according to Scripture that in God's providence, He permits everything that happens in our lives, whether suffering, tragedies, or blessings, "...God used it for good" accomplishing both temporal and eternal benefits. So the next time you experience something ranging from good to horrific, remember "we know that" it may or may not be a good thing that's happening, but it's working out for our good.

Application:

What are ways you can help yourself remember it's all working out for my good?

DAY 6

ARE YOU BURNING

When you set yourself on fire, people love to come and see you burn. — **John Wesley**

If someone walked up to you right now and took your temperature, what would they discover? Or, if they looked at your life through the lens of passion-goggles, would they see a person on fire? Take a moment to look at your life, or maybe ask someone, am I burning? We too often allow life to get us off track. Life happens! I want to give a few practical things to help restore that passion.

First of all, it is wise and important to pray for fire. You cannot start a fire in your church, home, community if you are not the first one burning. Secondly, make sure you have a good fireplace. Too often we try to live this life alone, when we were designed to live amongst the community. God spoke to Adam's situation and said it is not good to be alone. Obviously, contextually He was referring to a mate, but it is still not good to be alone in life. No person is an island! The writer of Hebrews says, "not forsaking our own assembling together" because it stimulates and encourages us. Thirdly, it is imperative that you focus your fire. Paul wrote to the Romans that some had misguided zeal, not in accordance with knowledge (Romans 10:2). Thus, it is imperative that you focus your fire on the thing that matters most to you. Fourth, fan your fire often. Paul writes to Timothy to stir up the gift, which means to keep the fire alive. Fire needs stoking in order to keep going. It is necessary to stoke the timbers from time to time. 1) God uses Himself to breathe on your flame 2) God uses people also. As "Iron sharpens iron, so does one man sharpen another" (Pv. 27:17) We all know that when iron connects with iron, sparks ignite. Surround yourself with key people that can affect your flame.

A person on fire changes their surrounding environment. A person with no passion is like a barber with no clippers, a ball player with no ball, or a river with no water. Bill Cosby once said, "Anyone can dabble, but once you've made that commitment...it's very hard for people to stop you" When I was younger my parents would often echo the words, "discover that which you would do for free, and pursue that in life." So I close in the words of my Father, "Pursue Your Passion. Contend for the faith. Make a great day."

Father, help us to burn bright for your glory. Amen

DAY 7

BE STILL AND KNOW

Oftentimes we find ourselves exhausted after facing difficult times in life. We can't find any energy to keep on going. Or maybe we are simply discouraged or too busy. We have to realize that we cannot do it alone, and if we continue to allow things to pile up on our plates, it will eventually get the best of us. There is a word of hope for us in the Scriptures, "God is with us" (Psalm 46:11). Whenever it seems as if the world is against you or the odds are stacked up high, "be still and know that I am God" rings loudly as a reminder that if you be still, not lazy, you can know God as a personal and powerful refuge. Whatever is your opposition or foe, it has to go through the Godhead. Despite your tight places (trouble) He will be a very present help (right now) speedily, and his help is permanent unlike the Earth, mountains, etc. We can also be still and know God as a river, which is symbolic of the refreshment he brings to us. This is in contrast to the threatening fast-moving waters of verse 3 (e.g. though its waters roar and be troubled). Lastly, we can be still and know God as the ruler that He is. Verse 10 gives us a call to action, a call to believe in Him (i.e. "know that I am God") First it's a call to believe in Him as a person ("I am"), Secondly, a call to believe He has a plan ("I will be exalted") and that plan is a victory. Thirdly, the Scripture gives us a call to believe in His presence "The Lord of hosts is with us") lastly, we find a call to believe in His power ("Our refuge").

Application:

What do you need to surrender to the Lord? Will you be still and know Him to be who He is?

DAY 8

ABC'S OF CREATIVITY

"Creativity is the joy of not knowing it all" (Ernie Zelinski).

Are you a Creative Presenter? Simply put a creative presenter is someone who seeks to present things creatively. Creativity is seeing more solutions than problems; yet, creativity is hard work and requires diligence. Prayerfully these few ABCs will aid in your process to become more creative also.

A) Arouse Questions

When planning events or thinking of new ways of doing things, I often encourage myself as well as those around me to poke holes in the boat, or arouse questions. My philosophy is we must always challenge the process. Someone once said, "if it's not broke then don't fix it" but why not re-train yourself to think "if it's not broke, break it and build it back up again." This is the difference between a quick life span or lengthens one. I once learned from reading Advanced Strategic Planning by Aubrey Malphurs that everything has a 1) Birth 2) Growth 3) Plateau 4) Decline and 5) Death. Thus, it is imperative to create a new beginning before that idea, vision, or event plateaus and eventually begins to decline and die.

B) Break Some Rules

I have heard all my life that creative people think outside the box, but I would like to submit to you that truly creative people not only think within the box, but find ways to use the outside of the box to accomplish their purposes. The box can often represent limitations, negativity, or other things that seek to hinder us; to that I say burst forth. But in this case the box represents rules, and they are meant to be learned and followed. However, in some cases those who have experienced great successes have known the rules and for a dramatic presentation broke them for emphasis. Broaden Your Horizon. Read. Learn. Discover. Execute.

C) Chop it up with Crea-ples

CREA-ples? I had been waiting to unveil this compound word until now. A Crea-ple is a person who is creative or better put creative people. What I have learned in my life is hanging with other crea-ples have done wonders in my creativity process. Some of my best works has been in collaboration with others whether through dialogue or their creative works. I constantly look at things from an approach of 1) what was done well (keep it) and 2) what was done poorly (improve it). I have also found to be true, some of the best crea-ples in this world are children. Children's minds are not bound by the risk, rules, and or results. They simply create. Spend more time with crea-ples, they just might be your own kids.

D) Develop Salubrious Settings

Charlie Bower once said, "A New idea is delicate. It can be killed by a sneer or a yawn; it can be stabbed to death by a quip and worried to death by a frown on the right man's brow." I am grateful that I have had people in my life to push me always. My number one love language is words of affirmation. Words from the right person can kill me or excite me. I remember hearing my father and/or mother telling me they loved me or thought highly of my accomplishments, and they strengthen me to go forward. To this day, when my father tells me how proud he is of me, I shed invisible tears of satisfaction. I know all too well about developing an environment promoting healthy creativity. Thus, I am very cautious of who I allow into my inner circle because I have to Eliminate Exterminators!

E) Eliminate Exterminators

Although the words from a few individuals could wound me deeply, I have learned how to eliminate exterminators who seek to devalue creativity and me. I fight hard to prove people wrong in so many aspects. One of my favorite poems is Somebody Said that it Couldn't Be Done because it seems to describe me. When someone says it can't be done, I buckle up! I chuckle! I reply! A few exterminators that I have discovered are 1) noise {nay-sayers} 2) pressure {deadlines or pressure from others to do something} 3) multitasking 4) procrastination {many times this is a fear of the unknown, failure, or rejection} 5) self-esteem {thinking you are not good enough} 6) Lexus trap {thinking you have to have the money in place before you begin}.

61

My ultimate point in presenting this blog is not to be an exhaustive account on creativity, but to challenge you to become more creative. For as we saw earlier, "Creativity is the joy of not knowing it all" but excitement in the discovery process. Become a CREA-PLE today!

Application:

How can you improve your creativity? What strategy stood out for you?

DAY 9

CARPE DIEM

I once heard "an opportunity of a lifetime must be seized in the lifetime of the opportunity." I believe that greatness lies within each of us, and we all have something to add of value to our generation; however, many within our generation don't rise to the opportunities that are presented them. Will you take advantage of your opportunities?

Now the truly great ones realize that every opportunity (small or big) they encounter could be the only opportunity they have, and that seized opportunity is preparation for something greater. Those who want to teach masses, are you teaching the one? Those who want to tour the world playing music, will you tour your city (nursing homes, small churches, schools, etc.). My Father stated to me countless times as an adolescent, "proper preparation prevents poor performance" and it's in the seizure of these small opportunities that can prepare you for greater ones.

Dr. King was one that seized many small opportunities throughout his tenure in college and as a young adult; therefore, when a great opportunity knocked he was prepared and walked confidently through the doors. Carpe Diem, or seize the day; stop robbing our generation of the wealth within you...Be Great and Make A Great Day!!! Grace and Peace!!!

Father God, give us wisdom on seizing each day for your glory and help us to redeem the time. Amen

DAY 10

BREAK ME OFF SOME PEACE

We live in a society where there is always something pulling at us and although it is true that stress can affect emotions, health, etc. No one can avoid stress. Everyone has some amount of stress each and every day. Stress is a typical reaction to demands made upon the body, it is normal and in some aspects needed part of life (i.e. when working out it is my goal to cause tension within my body so that my muscles can work and grow). Sadly enough many of us do not know how to manage stress, and it is the prolonged period of stress upon our bodies, emotions, etc. that can prove to be detrimental.

Paul tells us to "be anxious for nothing" (Phil. 4:6). Oftentimes, we as humans stress over things out of our control. I once heard that worrying about yesterday causes depression, and worrying about tomorrow causes anxiety. The exhortation by Paul is to be anxious for nothing, but pray. My father always said that prayer is the vehicle by which we communicate to God. You see rather than reacting to life's circumstances with worry, we should respond to life's circumstances with prayer, supplication, and requests with all thanksgiving. Thus, we can enjoy the peace of God, which is the inner calm or tranquility provided by the Father, and that transcends all human intellect, analysis, and/or insight, which shall be a protector of our heart and mind.

Stress can give us the energy and focus we need to deal with the situation, and it can motivate us to change. But too much stress can build up and cause us to worry, lose sleep or make choices that are not healthy. It is imperative that you and I "be anxious for nothing" but in everything let us pray. When we are anxious for nothing and respond to life's quagmires with communication with God, we will experience not only the peace with God (that all believers experience at salvation – Rom 5) but will also enjoy the peace of God.

Application:

How do you deal with stress? Have you spoken to the Father today? How much time do you spend in communication to God each day? How do you remind yourself of things to think about?

DAY 11

CLOSE ASSOCIATION WITH SIN!!!

After the death of Joshua, the Israelites did not completely obey the Lord. The tribes of Israel went into battle and where to drive out the inhabitants completely. They disobeyed the command and allowed the wicked inhabitants to remain. These inhabitants practiced everything from idolatry to immorality and through intermingling and intermarrying these lax spiritual standards filtrated its way into the moral fiber of the tribes of Israel, and they too became disobedience and lax spiritually. It was earlier in Deuteronomy that God predicted the gods of the Canaanites would become a hindrance to the spiritual walk of the people, and just as God predicted that is exactly what took place. The people disobeyed and reaped the devastation from it. What we should learn from their example is that too close association with sinful practices of the world will corrupt us, and we must totally separate ourselves from sin.

Application:

What are you holding on to that is contrary to God's standard of truth?

DAY 12

BREAKAWAY

"Take A Risk. Take A Chance. Make A Change. And Breakaway" - Kelly Clarkson

Many times people will find themselves rushing into their 30s, 40s, and sometimes into their 50s before they begin to gain a sense of purpose. I am convinced that the older one gets, the more the question of "why I exist" becomes more important to answer. Many people find themselves working and chasing the "American dream" or "chasing the jones" family (whoever they are) and never taking into consideration the reason they are on this planet. What is the wealthiest place on Earth? Quite possibly the wealthiest place on the Earth is in the graveyards, whereby you will find countless people who did not accomplish or reach their full potential.

Potential is untapped power...it is things you have yet to do.... it is all that you have not yet become....Myles Munroe once said, "potential is the sum of who you are that you have yet to reveal." I have known for a long time what I wanted to do in life, but as I got older that became fine-tuned. When I turned 25, I understood the value of creating a map for my life. This map would assist me in determining what I should engage in or not. My life map enables me to "take a risk, take a chance, make a change, and breakaway" from some things.

Even when you have to do certain jobs to get by for now, make sure you never lose sight of why you are here and how you are to fulfill that duty. Or maybe you should "take a risk, take a chance, make a change, and breakaway." Having a life map also helps you in identifying people who should be in your life (i.e. relationships, friends, etc.). Thus, you may have people you need to breakaway from because they possibly hinder you in the pursuit of your progression.

Application:

What is your life map? What guides you? What is your passion? Why do you exist? What special gifting or talents do you possess? Will you maximize your potential? I implore you to not rob our generation of the wealth and resource God has placed within you! Remember, sometimes you have to "take a risk, take a chance, make a change, and breakaway" in order to navigate your way through your life.

DAY 13

DISTRACTED BY GOOD.

As believers, we have many responsibilities that are appropriate and if allowed can occupy our time. Many believers occupy roles as parents, spouses, children, employees, etc. However, there are times when what is considered good can get in the way of that which is far better. Jesus enters the home of Mary and Martha, where Martha found herself involved in that which was good; she was serving. It was considered an honor to have the Son of God as the guest of honor, and she most likely wanted to see to it that the home was tidy and He felt welcome. However, that which was good got in the way of that which is far better. That which was well distracted Martha, but Mary was disciplined for that which was better; she sat at the Master's feet.

Application:

Are we distracted by the cares of this world? Are we distracted by our duties as spouses, parents, employees, etc.? Or are we disciplined enough to seek that which is better and needed? There is nothing wrong with our "good" duties, however, we must remember to "seek first the kingdom of God and righteous (His way of doing things), and all these other things will be added to you" (Matt 6:33)

DAY 14

I RUN

The writer of Hebrews emphasizes that our life of faith is described as a race, whereby a cloud of witnesses that give witness to the value and blessing of living by faith surrounds us. John Macarthur says, "Motivation for running 'the race' is not in the possibility of receiving praise from 'observing' heavenly saints;" however, as Christians there should be an external impulse to live our lives creatively much as the godly examples of those before us did. When we seek to travel behind the footsteps of others who have successfully run, there are three things necessary as presented in the text.

1) *Lay some things aside* – The runner that seeks to win loses as much as possible so that it won't hurt performance. The runner wears clothing that is light and allows freedom of movement. In the race of faith, we also lay aside things 1) weight 2) the sin. We lay aside things that may slow down our progress. We lay down relationships that aren't't beneficial and things that make our race difficult. We also lay aside the sin that easily ensnares us. This refers directly to the "sin of unbelief" which began this section in Hebrews (10:26). We cannot expect to

run successfully if we do not believe, and more importantly have faith in the Lord to accomplish all things.

2) *Push, Push and Push* – this race is not a sprint but a marathon and requires patience. We must run with a sustained effort over a long period, the race that is set before us. It is imperative to run the race set before you by the Lord Himself. Also, we don't run the stages in the race we have finished already, rather we run the course set before us today.

3) *Get Your Eye Right* – Our focus must be upon the Lord as we run the race. Oftentimes we glance at others but it should merely be a glance and not a gaze because our ultimate focus is on the author and finisher of our faith. Others can give expertise and wisdom, but our focus should be on the Lord and his example. I once read the formula for spiritual success is

1. If you want to be distressed – look within
2. If you want to be defeated – look back
3. If you want to be distracted - look around
4. If you want to be dismayed - look ahead
5. If you want to be delivered – look up.

Jesus is our supreme example of the willingness to suffer in obedience to the Lord. He pushed forward so that He might receive the joy of finishing His race in accordance with the will of the Father. Therefore, we look up to Him and run, run, run. Run the race set before you by laying aside unbelief, hindrances and things that slow down overall progress. Run the race before you with endurance, and run with absolute focus on the Lord Jesus.

Application:

Have you lost endurance in running your race? Have you grown weary in running? Are you focusing on the opinions of others or fixed on the ultimate prize? Have you been sidelined by unbelief? Let's Chop it up, and Join the conversation below!

DAY 15

DILIGENT OR LAZY

A few years back I developed this motto that has kinda stuck with me, "Make Moves." It was a call of motivation to put one foot forward and get to stepping. Oftentimes, we get complacent and comfortable, and that comfort turns into laziness, and if not careful we look up and see our lives passing by us. Proverbs gives an incredible amount of teaching concerning this, and I want to take a moment to share with you a small sampling.

- The diligent become rich, whereas the lazy becomes poor (Pv. 10:4)
- The diligent gathers early and considered to be wise, whereas the lazy sleeps during the day and causes shame (Pv. 10:5)
- The diligent will be satisfied, but the lazy follows frivolity. (Pv. 12:11)
- The diligent will rule, but the lazy will be alienated and forced into labor (Pv. 12:24)
- The diligent love to awake and eat, but the lazy loves to sleep and remains poor. (Pv. 20:13)

- The diligent makes careful plans and it leads to abundance, but the lazy makes hasty plans (Pv. 21:5)
- The diligent reaps abundance through hard work, but the lazy reap poverty for following frivolity. (Pv. 28:19)

Application:

The Bible is very clear concerning the diligent and the lazy man. Therefore, which are you? In what areas of your life do you need to become more diligent?

DAY 16

"IT IS NOT GOOD FOR MAN TO BE ALONE"
(Genesis 2:18)

When God saw man before the completion of the sixth day and creation of woman, He announced it was not good for man to be alone. Though God saw His creation good and even very good, yet in viewing the state of man God pronounced it was not good. Pointing to the inadequacy of man; he was incomplete without someone to properly complement him. Notice a few observations:

1) At this point, there is no sin
2) God and man have perfect communion, yet
3) God told man, that being alone was not good.

Now I know exegetically this passage is speaking about the marriage covenant, but I can hear the singles shouting right now... "Thank you Jesus...it is not good being alone." This world has everything catered toward couples. As much as we tell people to trust in God, it is possible that there is a void that 1) only God can fill, and 2) only humans can fill. My point in writing this blog is not to focus on marriage per se, but to focus on the value of human relationships. In the book DNA of Relationships, Gary Smalley says, "you were made for relationships." We have relationships of all kinds; family, friends, co-workers, etc. The secular world gathers at stadiums, Starbucks, and on the strip to feel connected. Many within the body of Christ are disconnected. We live in a society full of mass vehicles of communications yet we communicate less and less. We have become dislocated body parts. I believe that we must continue to develop a community. The writer of Hebrews urges us to not forsake our gathering together, for when we fellowship we provoke each other to love and good deeds. (Heb 10:24-25).

I once read "the church is where authentic community can take place." If you think about it, hardly anyone wants to be isolated; in fact, even those who live in rural areas find themselves meeting with people on some level. Why is this? We were made for relationships. We cannot escape it! No one just appears on earth; it takes all sorts of relationships for you to come into existence. Many of you who are reading this blog have found yourself becoming an isolationist, and those who fall into this rut are thieves. Yes, you are a thief, because you are robbing our generation of the gifts and talents deposited in you. Can you imagine the cure for cancer either walks on this Earth or lies in a grave? Many live and die without serving our generation and in many graves lay the various cures, musicians, prolific thinkers, etc. The bible says about David that after he had served his generation well he fell asleep (Acts 13:36).

Not even plants can grow unless in the midst of soil. Where is your good soil? Where are you planted? Who is in your community? The writer of Hebrews says, "And let us consider how to stir up one another to love and good works," (Hebrew 10:24 ESV) Notice that this passage is written to a group or community of Hebrew Christians whose attraction to Christ was in danger of eroding. For they were considering reverting back to the Levitical system of Judaism to avoid the persecution of following Solus Christus (Christ Alone). Therefore, mutual encouragement for them was vital for full commitment. The writer says, "stir up" which evokes inciting someone to something, such as love and good works. Lastly, the writer said to not forsake the assembling because corporate worship is imperative to our spiritual life. Notice the passage says, "and the more as we see the day approaching" (Hebrews 10:25). One of the master thinkers of our time is a guy name Francis Shaeffer, who wrote one of my favorite books A Christian Manifesto. Profound. In his book he says, "our relationship with each other is the criterion the world uses to judge whether our message is truthful for Christian community is the final apologetic."

Remember it is easier for a predator to prey on a sheep separated from the flock. Easier for the wind to knock down a tree alone. There is always strength in numbers. So whether you are married or single, remember God wants you to be among others, so that you can be provoked and provoke others to love and good deeds. All that God has placed in your life is for the benefit of the entire church, not just for your life. SE7EN!

Application:

What are ways we can be surrounded in community? Are you planted in good soil? Are you doing life with others of the same faith?

DAY 17

IF...

If I were taller, I would be rocking stages across the globe with my phenomenal ball skills. I would be endorsed by the greatest sports brand this generation has ever seen, embodying the slogan because I Did It!

IF I were faster, I would probably be on some track or field, with artificial turf playing on Sundays. Being a symbol of hope for some inner city kid, desiring to make it one day.

If I were smarter, I would be creating the newest technology to change the culture, or creating Jobs for Steve and them. If I was smarter I would be President and living a dream not deferred. I would know just how to manage people, time, and resources.

If I were "handsomer," I would be featured in the latest magazines, big screens, small screens, and various ads. I would take pictures from my best side: the front.

But What If...I didn't live my life in the if but the since. Since I AM who God created me to be, why don't I be all I was designed to be? Since I AM tall, I can stand as an example of an individual who took the cards he was dealt and played a great hand. Since I AM fast, be an example of an individual that sought the Lord wholeheartedly today and not tomorrow. Since I AM smart, use that wit to learn more and teach well. Since I AM handsome, become a walking billboard for the Lord. Allowing my worship to be the flyer to the main attraction.

I encourage you to not be bound by the IF, but be free by the SINCE. Look at all God made you to be and find out ways to live well because of that. It is easy to live in the what if, but how many of you will take the challenge and live despite your shortcomings.

From IF to SINCE!!!!!

Application:

What is your if? How can it become your since?

DAY 18

FACE YOUR GIANTS

For many of us, each year brings about the same progression of purposeful pursuits. For some we enter this New Year with apprehensive dreams, goals, and new perspectives as to what we want to accomplish. However, there is one thing we see in our near future that can cause problems in accomplishing these goals and dreams: A Giant. Either this giant is in your near future, or this giant has plagued you for many days, weeks, or years. This giant can come in the form of naysayers, low self-esteem (a false view of self), or even others trying to dictate what you do and how you do it. You are weary, weighed down and been waiting for inspiration or permission to get started with accomplishing your dreams. Here is a clue as to when to begin: NOW!!!!

The young shepherd boy David was also faced with a giant in the path of him becoming king. In the 16th chapter of 1 Samuel David was anointed as king. He had a positional blessing that wasn't manifested in practice yet, or better yet he was anointed for something and had not yet walked in it. Many of us also have things that God has anointed us for, but we have not yet seen the fulfillment of them. In order to not over spiritualize this statement, let's simply say that there are some dreams and goals that we see, but for whatever reason there is something blocking you from reaching them. In fact, there are some things in your life that you are trying to accomplish that no one else can or will accomplish. Look at Saul as an example, it is worthy to note that Saul, whose height was emphasized earlier in the text as being "from the shoulders up there was no man found taller" (1 Sam 9:2) and yet was not found courageous enough to accept the challenge to slay the giant. Many of you reading this find yourself in a similar position, for you are a trail blazer to break the cycle of illiteracy, the cycle of entitlement, the cycle of not pursuing your dreams. You may not stand as tall as Saul or others in your family, circle, community, etc. but you are brave enough to pursue those dreams and slay the giant.

This year it is my prayer that you see the incredible potential inside of you. I remember as a 1st year college student reading Myles Munroe's books on Potential, he submits that potential is places you have not gone that you can go, dreams you have not dreamed that you can dream, or things you can do that you have yet to do. Remember the only way to eat an elephant is to take one bite at a time, the only way to climb a mountain is to take one step at a time, the only way to drive a stick shift is to change one gear at a time, and the only way to slay a giant is to make a decision to face it. Don't be one of the 10 spies (Numbers 13) who saw the giants in Canaan and "saw themselves" as grasshoppers in the giants' sight, but see yourself as the only 2 spies that saw themselves as over comers. Notice, the 10 spies came back and saw themselves as grasshoppers in the sight of the giants - how often do you assume how someone else sees you? How often do you allow others to detour you? David looked at the uncircumcised giant as opposition and saw him as so big he couldn't miss.

One last lesson I would like to emphasize in this passage. Before David faced the giant, Saul interviews him and in many ways has similarities to Goliath. Saul is found placing His trust in his military experience and strong armor (1 Sam 17: 31-40) yet he lacked the courage to stand up to Goliath. After hearing the resume of David, Saul agrees to let this young boy go fight a grown man's battle. Saul places his armor on David, and he could barely move. Oftentimes people place on you pressures, expectations, and other things that they themselves couldn't even fulfill. We have to remove those things and fight the battle God gives us the way He wired us to fight it. As God spoke to Moses, "what is that in your hand?" (Ex 4:2), he could be symbolically speaking to us "what is that in your hand?" "What have I placed in you?" As John C Maxwell puts it "keep moving forward on the journey, making the best of the detours and interruptions, turning adversity into advantage." Begin to tell your giant of low self-esteem, giant of low math skills, giant of poverty, etc. that "Today the Lord will conquer you, and I will kill you and cut off your head." Overcoming your giant on the path to your dreams and goals being fulfilled can be an incredible witness to the world of who your God is. One writer stated that "David's conquest over Goliath revealed the power that one faithful man could possess—the man with the kind of heart God looked for (13:14; 16:7)"

Application:

What is your dream? What are you praying to accomplish this year? Pursue your passion! Ask yourself, why not me? Why not today? - SE7EN

GILLIGAN'S ISLANDS CHRISTIANS

"Just sit right back and you'll hear a tale, a tale of a fateful trip that started from this tropic port aboard this tiny ship..." (Gilligan's Island Theme Song)

Do you recall this song? These few words are the beginning of an interesting song that pretty much gave everyone an idea as to how castaways got stranded on an isle. What I find most fascinating about this sitcom, namely Gilligan's Island is that every episode was filled with DRAMA. There was always something happening with this crew, from gossip to fights, to someone snooping in someone else's business. Now I mind you I am over 30 years of age and I don't remember everything about this show, but I do remember the DRAMA. I couldn't tell you what episode or who did what, but what I do know is that these were some characters. They used all this time, effort, and energy to fight, fuss, and gossip rather than finding a way to get off the island. Another thing is that these people created so much stuff with some bamboo. I mean they had created beds, frames for their huts, a pipe, weapons, bowling alley, and bikes (for cleaning clothes, etc.). I mean come on now....you mean to tell me, that you could create all this stuff and couldn't create a boat to sail away. Now I know this is TV, but oddly enough I see Christians fitting this picture oh too well. We are so consumed with building our personal dynasties and luxuries that we can't find ways to build the kingdom of God. We are so concerned with health, wealth, and prosperity that we are turning our attention directed towards the Lord to the Earth (Matt 6:21) Also, too many Christians are consumed in gossip, slander, fighting, and debating over non-essential issues that we are not focusing our energy on the lost. Let's fight for the lost. Let's fight for the kingdom. Let's not fight for our own agendas. Notice something about light. Light in and of itself can light a room, corner, or city. However, that same light when it is focused or streamlined can become a laser. A regular light source emits in all directions and over a widespread area. A laser emits through a specific location, which can cut through the hardest of objects. If we focus our lights we too can pierce the toughest objects. Let's get to "lasering"

Remember the words of Paul, "Woe to me if I preach not the gospel..." (1 Cor 9:16)

Father, may we be more consumed by building your kingdom than building our individual ones. Amen

DAY 20

SUPPORT SYSTEMS

A man who is dealing with unemployment, uncertainty, and misunderstandings takes his own life...A mother of several kids is doing it all alone and in over her head, feels she has no hope and murders her kids and herself...The pastor of a small church teaching sound doctrine closes down after several years because lack of support...A business owner invests life earnings and no one comes and is forced to close business... An ex-con tries to do it by the book, seeking to turn his life around, but continues to hear rejection turns to the only thing he knows to make a living...

Oftentimes we see people who throw in the towel, and we wonder "why?" If only we would become proactive and not reactive, we may just be the support that person needed to go a little further. My Father tells a story about a pastor who met with a couple. They were experiencing hard times and the pastor begin to pray one of those "super spiritual" prayers... "Father, I pray you bless this couple. I pray that you provide all their needs according to your riches and glory in Christ Jesus...I decree and declare that their needs will be met..." Meanwhile, as he was praying, the pastor felt a tug of the heart and the voice of God saying "what they need is in your pocket." The pastor quickly ended the prayer and reached into his pocket to bless the couple.

So often the support (prayer, provision, and participation) is within our reach and capability; if you only would be sensitive enough to the Spirit of God and become more proactive instead of reactive!!!! – Grace and Peace #Transform

Application:

What are some ways we can become more supportive? What are examples of how a person could support the individuals listed above?

DAY 21

LAYING HOLD

"...forgetting those things which are behind me and reaching forward to those things which are ahead." (Phil. 3:13)

Many Christians have a hard time forgetting where and going beyond where they have come from. This is past of sin, failure, etc. and to be honest it is very hard sometimes moving past it. They are sorry for the mistakes they have made and came seem to do what Jesus has already done for them; Forgive Themselves!!!

Paul strained with everything in him to lay hold of maturity. I think it is good to remember that the pursuit of Christlikeness starts with an honest review of where you are not and dissatisfaction with being there. "I haven't arrived at the place of maturity for which Christ saved me." Then it's about pushing forward. The Christian life is a progressive day-by-day thing. We mature progressively until one day we are finally home with the Father.

Application:

Are you straining? Have you made an honest assessment with where you are? Are you dissatisfied with where you are currently? Will you do what is necessary to lay hold of the ultimate prize?

DAY 22

SECRET MILLIONAIRES

There is a show on television, entitled Secret Millionaire. This show is about millionaires who go undercover to work in their companies and ultimately give away thousands of dollars to the employees they work along in need. While watching this, I begin to dream. I begin to think immediately, "if only I had a million dollars how much I would give and assist others." In mid-thought, I believe the Lord caused a seismic earthquake of the heart. I begin to think back over my life when I have said similar things. I thought about when I would dream of winning, finding, or inheriting millions and all I would do for the kingdom of God (i.e. churches built, restored, people to assist, etc.). However, I would often be nudged by the Spirit of God as if to speak to my heart saying "Robert, you don't have to be a millionaire to become a giver, but being a cheerful giver you are more than a millionaire; you are loved by God and given more to sow". I would like to share two points out of 2 Corinthians 9 for support:

1) God loves a cheerful giver

Whomever God loves, He looks after. For God so loved the world, He looked after us by providing His only son (John

3:16). Because God looks after those He loves, the cheerful giver has nothing to worry (Matthew 6:33). David wrote in the Psalms that the Lord delivers out of trouble, them that give to the poor (Ps. 41:1-3) Also note that the harvest is directly proportionate to the seed sown.

2) God gives seed to the sower

I love the verse found in 2 Corinthians 9:10 and think many people look right over it. The verse enlightens the reader that the sower receives more seed to sow. This should help us in our thinking; that rather than waiting to become a millionaire to give, we should become Secret Millionaires in our own right. As a former struggling college student, I know all too well the importance of financial assistance. I would love to walk into a bursar's office and put money towards a deserving student's financial account, or assist a struggling family with bills, food, etc. But why do we have to dream big and stop at reality? Why not dream big and work our way to the desired reality? If it is our desire to become secret millionaires, we should start today as secret millionaires and begin to sow bountiful seeds that will one day produce a bountiful harvest. Remember God gives seed to the sower, which the individual who is known by his is sowing, thus continuing the cyclical effects; the more we give, the more God will enable us to give.

Application

Our gifts should be given liberally (Rom. 12:6-8), cheerfully (2 Cor. 9:6) and purposefully (2 Cor. 9:7), because as we continue to read in 2 Corinthians 9, our giving produces thanksgiving and glory to God (2 Cor 9:11-15) and increases the fruits of our righteousness (2 Corinthians 9:10b). Not everyone has the treasures to give away, but we can all give either time or talent. You may not be able to give to support a student's tuition bill, but you may be able to buy a textbook or two. You may not be able to pay a church member's bill, but you may have the income to buy a week's worth of groceries. You may not even be able to give financially, but you have skills, trades, or talents to assist in something for someone. My Father used to teach always giving according to your faith and watch how God increases the level of your faith and resources. Thus, I encourage you to start where ever you are able to give cheerfully and over time your seeds will become bigger and bigger. Remember, "God is able to make ALL grace ABOUND to you, so that having ALL sufficiency in ALL things at ALL times, you may ABOUND in every good work" (2 Corinthians 9:8).

In what ways do you see yourself applying this? Is your heart enthusiastically thrilled with the pleasure of giving? How do you need God's grace to abound toward you?

FIRE OF COALS: A PLACE OF REGRET AND RESTORATION

In John 21:9 it says, "then, as soon as they had come to land, they saw a fire of coals there, and fish laid on it, and bread." Now many of you are probably thinking, "ok, so what is the big deal?" I am glad you asked that question. If you remember, it was surrounding a fire of coals that the student leader of the 12 disciples denounced Jesus. The bible declares in the gospel of John that the men where around a fire of coals when a servant girl asked if Peter was with Jesus. He denied her such that he emphatically cursed her out. Jesus forewarned Peter that the enemy wanted to sift him out as wheat (Luke 22:31), yet when he was restored to strengthen his brothers.

Here we have Jesus using the very scenario whereby Peter denounced him (a fire of coals) restoring Peter to prominence. Jesus took the very situation that brought Peter shame and used it as a springboard to him strengthening his brothers. Many of us have gone through shameful moments, situations, quagmires, or predicts and that may as well be the very thing(s) Jesus use to bring us to a place of prominence. However, in the process of restoring Peter we still find a problem in the story. The next few verses show the limitations to the English language. Jesus takes Peter aside and asks him a question, "Peter, lovest thou me more than these?" And Peter answers, "Yea, Lord, thou knowest that I love thee" Now from the naked eye you might say, "what's the issue?" However, a closer look at the text and we see that the word for love used by these two men are drastically different. Jesus uses the word agapao (agape) and Peter uses phileo. Jesus ask "do you have the greatest form of love for me?" and Peter replies, "Yes Lord I am fond of you" This transpires twice before Jesus comes down to the level of Peter and says, "Peter are you fond (phileo) me" and Peter quips, "Lord you know all things."

The significance of the passage is that Jesus surrounding the fire of coals sought to restore Peter and had to come down to the level of Peter. Peter was not able to rise to the level of where Jesus was, but Jesus met him at the point of where he was. However, it was Peter in his first epistle (1 Peter 1:22) that writes about loving the brethren sincerely (Philadelphia) and having a deep love (agape) for one another. Peter, who couldn't reach the level at first and needed for Jesus to come down to his level, was restored and then able feed Jesus' sheep (John 21:17). So I write this to say, where ever you are in life, whatever your circumstance might be...realize that God will meet you at the point of where you are in order to bring you up to where He wants you to be. The very thing that brought you shame or disappointment might be your fire of coals, which turns out to be a place of restoration.

Application

How has God brought restoration in your life? How can you mirror the example of Christ to others? How has God shown His love for you in the midst of your shame?

DAY 24

MAN OF ENCOURAGEMENT!!!

Who is this man name, Joseph, a Levite from Cyprus? What makes him so important that the apostles called him Barnabas, which means son of encouragement? What did he do to earn such a phenomenal name?

Barnabas is introduced by Luke as a prominent role model and later became associated with Paul. If it weren't for Barnabas maybe we wouldn't have a ministry of Paul or even the Gospel According to Mark. For it was Barnabas who brought Saul to the apostles after his conversion. It was Barnabas who disagreed with Paul later and took John Mark under his wings and encouraged him. Despite his falling out with Paul, he lived up to his name and was "full of faith and the Holy Spirit" (acts 11:24).

I believe that we miss opportunities each and every day to be an encouragement to someone else. First of all, take a chance on someone. Who knows what the person discouraged can achieve with a simple word from you. Secondly, as seen in the life of Barnabas with Paul and John Mark, work along side of them. Barnabas helped Paul in using his gifts to accomplish great things. Next, we learn from Barnabas to give others another chance. We see countless examples of people throughout Scripture that were given additional chances; therefore, we should reciprocate that to others. We should also cease to hold resentment against people. Beacue of Barnabas taking a chance on John Mark, we see the gospel according to Mark and we also see Paul writing to Timothy that John Mark was useful to him now. Lastly, we should teach others also to encourage!!!

Application:

What ways can you apply these lessons? Are you an encourager? Can you identify 3 people to lavish encouragement and love on?

DAY 25

MAKING MOVES

Many times in our life it seems as if we are not making moves. It seems like we've been walking for days, months, and even years, but keep coming back to the same rock. God never intended for this journey to be a circular route. Our God never intended for us to walk in the Spirit via a treadmill. Rather our God wants us to grab hold to the vision and in the words of my college bible study's chant "Move baby Move."

Vision creates in you a mission and a contagious spirit that is felt by others, and they begin to walk alongside you. Long hours of labor are more than freely given to accomplish any feat. Many of us live our lives and all of a sudden catch the vision, but what happens when you put the pedal to the medal but your feet won't reach. You see "vision without resources was a hallucination" (Author Unknown) and "without a vision the people perish, or cast off restraint" (Prov. 29:18). Though this passage speaks of the revelation of the Word of God, many times it is through the hearing and application of the Word that we receive our "unique" vision for life. However, because of inadequate resources, the vision seems to be so out of grasp.

But one thing I know about vision….it will make you do some strange things. Vision will make a college student take 77 hours in 3 semesters while holding down a full time gig (ask Robert). Vision will make you live on noodles (ask college students) be a newsboy on trains (ask Thomas Edison) or start off making $4 a month (Andrew Carnegie). Did you know that John D. Rockefeller started off making $6 a week or that Julius Caesar was an epileptic? In the words of Helen Keller, "the worst thing than to be born blind is to live with no sight." John C. Maxwell says, "look within you, look behind you, look around you, look ahead of you, look above you, and look beside you." What do you feel? What have you learned? What is happening to others? What is the big picture? What does God expect of you? What resources are available to you?

One thing I know about God is when He gives you a vision, He will also give you provision. God will always give provision for His vision. Vision should always be greater than you. Jesus tells us "His grace is sufficient for us that in our weakness He is made perfect" (2 Cor. 12:9-10). This speaks volumes to me, for when I am trying to put the pedal to the medal but it seems my feet won't reach, my God will be like the little boy on Indiana Jones….you remember, He couldn't't reach the pedal, so He had wood blocks on his feet. Our God will be unto our feet like the wood blocks erasing the in from inadequate, or making the inadequacy a metaphor of the adequacy that is coming from with-IN you. For greater is He who is in you than He who is in the world (1 John 4:4).

A person with a vision gives a little talk but does a lot. A person with vision finds strength from inner convictions and continues when problems arise. Let us get to pursuing with all our might to advance the kingdom and watch God cover the rest. Your kingdom grind might not be like mine; in fact, I am sure it will not be. Whatever your niche is, grind it out for the kingdom wholeheartedly (Col. 3:23) and watch how God will give you sufficient grace for your insufficient resources. When you are frail, trust in God to enable you to prevail.

"MAKE MOVES"

Application:

What is your vision? What obstacles have you had to overcome to keep pushing forward? What measures are in place for you to accomplish your vision?

DAY 26

SERVE WELL!!!

We live in a world where nobody wants to be servants, in fact even those who embrace the term have to add to it and call themselves servant-leaders. I believe it is important to remind ourselves often to be servant and serve selflessly. There are three things I would love for you to consider this week as you serve. A true servant does not demand recognition. Servants are willing to remain in the shadows if need be. Jesus tells the audience during the greatest sermon ever preached, to not let your deeds be seen by others (Matthew 6:1-2). Also, a true servant does not demand rewards. A good rule of thumb is always give without expecting anything in return. Lastly, a true servant does not demand His rights. A servant has a submissive spirit to God and others. Service is the evidence of genuine love and it is love in action (1 Cor 9:9; 13:5). Serve at a level you have never serve before, serve well today!!!

Father, give us the heart of a servant, always seeking others above ourselves. Amen

DAY 27

REDEDICATION VS. SURRENDER

Each year countless people make New Year's Resolutions. You see much of this New Year's resolution stuff is a result of a person's habits getting out of hand. Therefore, for the New Year they begin to determine in their mind what they want to change. Whether it's losing weight, gaining, or some other goal, each year many people will make a list of goals (resolutions) in which they desire to accomplish. Many that will be long forgotten by the middle of the year.

This mindset has even crept into mainstream Christianity. Do you know the way Alaskans catch wolves? In essence, they are killed by their own blood as they are lying in the snow

This is how sin affects us. We are attracted to it because it satisfies the flesh (old patterns of getting our needs met apart from God), and before we know it, we have indulged our pleasures and we are now lifeless. Sin causes us to be separated from God. Believers don't lose relationship, but we do lose deep communion with God. You see belief systems create thought process that leads to emotions eventually becoming manifested sin in our lives. This sin if continued

109

becomes a habitual act, and a habit eventually becomes a stronghold and ultimately you are completely off course. Maybe you are in this position now and you are at church and the Lord convicts you through the man of God, and he asks for you to re-dedicate your life to God. However, what we are really saying many times is, "Lord, I will try hard."

When we re-dedicate our life to God, "it's as if we are saying, "I blew it last time, this time I will try harder." But the fact of the matter is that if we can do it, or try harder and succeed, there was no need for Jesus the Christ to come to this Earth. Jesus is the only one who could do it, or live the "life." We have to develop a mindset of telling God, "Lord, I cannot do it. I surrender my life unto you." For you see, "I have been crucified with Christ nevertheless I live, but not I Christ lives within me" (Gal. 2:20). "He made Him who knew no sin to become sin for us that we might become the righteousness of God" (II Cor. 5:21). It's what my father calls the great exchange! Jesus came to give His life for me, to give His life to me, to live His life through me. The fact is Christ cannot effectually live through me until I surrender my life unto Him. So, I implore you to stop trying harder and start surrendering today. Peace!!!

Application:

What do you need to surrender to the Lord? How can you become more available to the Lord?

DAY 28

STOP WORRYING
START PRAYING!!!!

So often in our lives we focus on things in our past. Instead of forgetting those things that are behind us (whether good or bad) we tend to go back and rehash memories, thus produces anxiety in our lives. Paul writes to the Church in Philippi and states "be anxious for nothing" or 'do not go back down memory lane, bringing back memories to rehash and, therefore, causing fear, doubt and uncertainty." Worrying in the life of the believer is really a person who is not trusting and relying upon God to meet all needs. As believers, we should place our full confidence and trust in the Lord's sovereignty, wisdom power and His care for us. Rather we should replace the weeds of doubt and uncertainty with the seeds of Scripture. "In His law I meditate both day and night and shall be like a tree planted…" (Ps 1). Paul tells us to not worry anything but rather pray everything. In doing so, the promise for an inner strength, calmness, and tranquility is realized in the believer even though it surpasses all human intellect. (Phil.4:4-6)

Application:

What have you been worrying about? Will you lay it at the altar? Will you begin to trust Father to meet your needs?

DAY 29

FINISH WELL

"2930 people are mentioned in the Bible by name, and of those, there are about 100 whose lives are followed. Of the hundred, only one-third finished well. The majority remaining failed in the second half of their lives." – Howard Hendricks

Have you ever seen a good movie that the end just didn't captivate you? I must be the first to say that movies like Sixth Sense, Arlington Road, Unbreakable, and Devil's Advocate are few and far between (good movies with good endings) but in life this is what we hope to ascertain. We hope to "Finish Strong!"

In my studies and presentations over the past few years I have learned that many have started well but many have not "Finished Well." In order to "Finish Well" I have learned 3 things from the Book of Corinthians I'd like to share with you (1 Cor 9:24-27). An individual must be committed to 1) Excellence 2) Endurance and 3) Integrity

1) Commitment to Excellence –

Do you start anything in life with the goal of being last? Paul here illustrates our spiritual walk to that of a race, which for the Corinthians wouldn't serve as a problem since the Ancient Greeks celebrated the Olympics and Isthmian games. Notice, 1) many run in the race but only one wins the prize 2) run in such a way that you may obtain it. Winning requires purpose and discipline! For Paul says, "for everyone who competes for the prize, is temperate in all things" (v.25). This means an individual must engage himself in strict training. In other words, Paul is saying to us if you want to receive the prize you must have self control, in fact you have to excel above everyone else.

2) Commitment to Endurance –

The Scriptures says, "everyone who competes for the prize..." or as King James says, "every man that striveth." The word in the Greek used for compete, or striveth, is the word agonizomai, whereby we get the word agonize. This word means, to contend, to endeavor with strenuous zeal. In other words, when competing for a prize you have to be patient, or suffer long. The New International Version calls this striving, "strict training" Two things you must realize 1) don't cut short your training 2) maintain an eternal perspective (get a crown that will last forever).

When a person has a goal in mind, they endure sweat and tears in order to accomplish their goal. They have to maintain a prize perspective. Ultimately you and I have to maintain an eternal perspective, because we are seeking an imperishable crown. Remember, endurance is unwavering resolve, or fortified tenacity that makes us keep going, regardless of the obstacles that might come into our life to slow us down or give up.

3) Commitment to Integrity –

In pursuit of the ultimate prize, we must be committed to integrity. Paul here tells the believers in Corinth that they have to have a commitment to integrity. Notice what he says in verse 26.... "Therefore, I run thus: not with uncertainty. Thus, I fight: not as one who beats the air" This metaphor is a picture of a shadow boxer who 1) waves his arms in the air and/or 2) a boxer who misses his opponent. Paul says that he is not an individual just waving his arms in the air and not connecting, but he is one who consistently make contact. The word integrity is a beautiful word when you break it down...think about it, what is the root word for integrity.... integrate/integer...both of these words has the understanding of wholeness. An integer is a mathematical term for a whole number and integrate pictures two sides becoming one. Therefore, integrity has to deal with becoming one. Integrity is your actions becoming one with what your mouth says. It is not professing to be a "Saint" and living like an "Aint." Integrity is professing Christ and possessing Him also. Paul says in the 27th verse that he disciplines his body and brings it into subjection.

Ultimately, we train ourselves to run the race, but let us not get sidetracked or slowed down. Let us keep our eyes on Jesus, the true goal. For living the Christian life demands all of our energy. Thus, we can forget about our past and strain for the prize because Christ promises eternity with Him at the race's end. FINISH WELL!!!!!!

Gal. 5:7 (ESV) "You were running well. Who hindered you from obeying the truth?"

Eccl. 9:11 (ESV) "Again I saw that under the sun the race is not to the swift, nor the battle to the strong..." *but to the one who endures to the end.*

DAY 30

SPRING FORWARD

Each year begins and I am sure many of you think in the words of Paul to the Philippians "Not that I have already obtained it or already become perfect" (3:12a) and that's great if you want to reach the prize. What is the prize you might ask? Well according to the passage the prize is spiritual perfection, or Christlikeness. However, I believe some key principles can be applied to life in general.

If a person wants to receive the prize, they must first have Proper Awareness of where or what you are not. Many of us have started this year off with keys goals in mind and to be honest 3 months in and we are not there. However, in order to reach the goal it requires Maximum Effort. Paul says, "But I press on so that I may lay hold of..." (3:12b) thus an individual will not reach the goal until they first realize the need to improve and then it takes a springing forth. Paul believed in total dependency on God's power to work in and through him (Col 1:29). Later in the same book Paul writes "I can do all things through Christ who infuses inner strength into me" (Phil 4:13 - paraphrase). Therefore, we lean and depend on the Lord to make it do what it do.

Many of us have faced our giant and moved beyond the obstacle that face us, but we have become stagnant thinking we have arrived, yet we have not reached the goal by which we set out to ascertain. We must Spring Forward and focus our attention on that which lies ahead. Notice Paul says, "... forgetting what lies behind and reaching (springing) forward to what lies ahead" (3:13). Springing forward, or reaching forward, translates as stretching a muscle to its limitations to reach a goal. In the movie "Rocky 4" the slogan that said it best was "no pain no gain;" therefore, we must push ourselves to the limit to reach the goal, because ultimately we are trying to make the Lord famous with our goals and aspirations. So as we Spring forward naturally, I pray that you use this time as a reminder to Spring Forward in your pursuit of the ultimate prize.

Application:

What are some things that hinder you from reaching your goals? What will you take away from this devotional? Have you made much progress? Where do you see yourself in the next 5 years?

DAY 31

PATIENTLY WAIT

I was once read somewhere "the worst thing than waiting is wishing you had." I don't know about you, but this quote blessed me. How many times have we jumped into a relationship, purchase, or something else only to regret we did as time elapsed? What I have learned is that patience is the unique way we allow deceit to rear its head; however waiting is very difficult. When we wait, it seems as if everything around us is progressing but us. Because of the benefits that come with waiting on God, we should patiently wait for him; God grants us answers, guidance, etc. when we wait upon the Lord. It is His desire that we wait for him for in doing so we acknowledge that He alone has the answers to our decisions. Thus, when we wait upon the Lord, our strength is renewed, and we walk in His wisdom.

Lord, teach us to wait on you. Amen

Join The Conversation

Blog @robertlwagner.com

Facebook @robertlwagner07

Twitter @robertlwagner

Instagram @robertlwagner

Youtube @robertlwagner

Robert L. Wagner is an artist, author, speaker and media personality. One of his generations most creative bible expositors and the "master of integration." He is a graduate of Dallas Theological Seminary and Lead Pastor-Teacher at Ark Bible Fellowship in Arlington, Tx. His blog, social media platforms and youtube channel draws countless viewers daily.

CPSIA information can be obtained at www.ICGtesting.com
Printed in the USA
LVOW11s1442230215

427997LV00001B/188/P